Abraham Coles

Dies iræ in 13 original versions

Abraham Coles

Dies iræ in 13 original versions

ISBN/EAN: 9783742842329

Manufactured in Europe, USA, Canada, Australia, Japa

Cover: Foto ©ninafisch / pixelio.de

Manufactured and distributed by brebook publishing software (www.brebook.com)

Abraham Coles

Dies iræ in 13 original versions

DIES IRÆ

IN

THIRTEEN ORIGINAL VERSIONS

BY
ABRAHAM COLES, M.D.

SECOND EDITION.

NEW YORK:
D. APPLETON AND COMPANY.
1860.

Entered according to Act of Congress in the year 1859, by
ABRAHAM COLES,
in the Clerk's office of the District Court of the District of
New Jersey.

RIVERSIDE, CAMBRIDGE:
STEREOTYPED AND PRINTED BY
H. O. HOUGHTON AND COMPANY.

INTRODUCTION.

IT would be difficult to find, in the whole range of literature, a production to which a profounder interest attaches than to that magnificent canticle of the Middle Ages, the DIES IRÆ. Fastening on that which is indestructible in man, and giving fitter expression than can elsewhere be found, to experiences and emotions which can never cease to agitate him, it has lost after the lapse of six centuries none of its original freshness and transcendent power to affect the heart. It has commanded alike the admiration of men of piety and men of taste. By common consent, it is as Daniel remarks: *sacræ poeseos summum decus et Ecclesiæ Latinæ κειμήλιον est pretiosissimum.* Among gems it is the diamond. It is solitary in

its excellence. Of Latin Hymns, it is the beſt known and the acknowledged maſterpiece. There are others which poſſess much sweetness and beauty, but this ſtands unrivalled. It has superior beauties, with none of their defects. For the moſt part they are more or less Romiſh, but this is Catholic, and not Romiſh at all. It is universal as humanity. It is the cry of the human. It bears indubitable marks of being a personal experience.

The author is supposed to have been a monk: an incredible suppoſition truly did we not know that a monk is also a man. One thing is certain, that the monk does not appear, and that it is the man only that speaks. He no longer dreams and drivels. He is effectually awake. The veil is lifted. He sees Chriſt coming to Judgment. All the tumult and the terror of the Laſt Day are present to him. The final pause and syncope of Nature; the ſhuddering of a horror-ſtruck Universe; the down-ruſhing and wreck of all things—all are present. But these material circumſtances of horror and amazement, he feels are as nothing compared with "the infinite terror of being found guilty before the Juſt Judge." This single consideration swallows up every other. The interests of an eternity are crowded into a moment.

One great secret of the power and enduring popularity of this Hymn is, undoubtedly, its genuineness. A vital sincerity breathes throughout. It is a cry *de profundis;* and the cry becomes sometimes—so intense are the terror and solicitude—almost a shriek. It is in the highest degree pathetic. The Muse is "Mater Lachrymarum, Our Lady of Tears." Every line weeps. Underneath every word and syllable, a living heart throbs and pulsates. The very rhythm, or that alternate elevation and depression of the voice, which prosodists call the *arsis* and the *thesis*, one might almost fancy were synchronous with the contraction and the dilatation of the heart. It is more than dramatic. The horror and the dread are real; are actual not acted. A human heart is laid bare, quivering with life, and we see and hear its tumultuous throbbings. We sympathize—nay, before we are aware, we have changed places. We, too, tremble and quail and cry aloud.

All true Lyric Poetry is subjective. The DIES IRÆ is, as we have seen, remarkable for its intense subjectivity; and whoever duly appreciates this characteriftic, will have little difficulty in underftanding its superior effectiveness over everything else that has been written on the same theme. The life of the writer has paffed into it and informs it, so that it is itself alive. It has vital forces and emanations. Its life mingles with our life. It enters into our veins and circulates in our blood. A virtue goes out from it. It is electrically charged, and contact is inftantly followed by a fhock and fhuddering.

Springing from its subjectivity, if not identical with it, we would further notice, the intenfifying effect of what may be called its personalism, in other words its ego-ism. It is I and not We. Subftitute the plural pronoun for the fingular, and it would lose half its pungency. We have had occafion to observe the weakening effect of this in tranflation. The truth is, the feeling is of a kind too concentrated and too exacting to allow itself to be diffipated in the vagueness of any grouping generality. The heart knoweth its own bitterness. There is a grief that cannot be fhared, neither can it be joined on to another's. It is not social nor common. It is mine and not yours. It is exclusive, not because it is selfish, but because it has depths beyond the soundings of ordinary sympathy.

This is especially true of some of the intenser forms of religious experience, proceeding as they do from that which is most intimate and innermost, the penetralia of a man's consciousness, his most secret and peculiar self. There is an inner and privileged sanctuary of the heart, which is kept as a chamber locked up. It is hidden and sacred. It may be, that the individual, dwelling habitually in the outer courts of his being, rarely if ever enters into it himself. For man is twofold. A veil divides between the outer and the inner man. Gross and sensual, the majority of mankind are averse to lifting the concealing medium, for fear of unwelcome revelations and discoveries respecting themselves. Goethe is an example of this portentous preference for half knowledge: "Man," he says, "is a darkened being; he knows not whence he came, nor whither he goes; he knows little of the world and less of himself. I know not myself, and may God protect me from it."

In conversion to God this veil is rent from top to

bottom. There is a self-revelation. Behind the curtain, there in the Moſt Holy Place, where ought to be the Shekinah, the ſhining, ſenſible Manifeſtation of the Divine Presence, he beholds the Abomination of Iniquity set up. He awakes to the ſtartling faƈt that he is "without God and without hope in the world." A voice of urgency is sounding in his ears: "Flee from the Wrath to Come." He anticipates the terrors of the Judgment. He feels that there is not a moment to lose. Inſtinƈt prompts, and the Word of God enjoins, that he seek to save himself firſt. He knows not whether others are in as bad a case as he. But of his own guilt and danger he has no doubt. An offended Maker confronts him, him in particular. So he prays and agonizes. His may not be "the thews which throw the world"—he is conscious of weakness rather than ſtrength—yet ſingly and alone, he wreſtles with God like Jacob, and prevails like Israel.

The Hymn is not only lyrical in its eſſence, but also in its form. It is inſtinƈt with muſic. It ſings itself. The grandeur of its rhythm, and the aſſonance and chime of its fit and powerful words, are, even in the ears of those unacquainted with the Latin language, suggeftive of the richeft and mightieft harmonies. The verse is ternary; and the ternary number, having been efteemed anciently a symbol of perfection and held in great veneration, may possibly have had something to do with the choice of the ftrophe. Be this as it may, its metrical ftructure, as all agree, conftitutes by no means the leaft of its extraordinary merits. Trench, in his Selections from Latin Poetry, speaks of the metre as being grandly devised, and fitted to bring out some of the nobleft powers of the Latin language; and as being, moreover, unique, forming the only example of the kind that he remembers. He notices the solemn effect of the triple rhyme, comparable to blow following blow of the hammer on the anvil. Knapp, in his Liederschatz, likens the original to a blaft from the trump of resurrection, and declares its power inimitable in any tranflation.

HISTORY OF THE HYMN.

THE authorship of the Dies Iræ is ascribed, apparently upon good grounds, to Thomas of Celano, so called from a small town of that name in Italy. He was a friend and pupil and subsequently the biographer of St. Francis of Assisi, the founder of the order of Minorites, (called also Friars-Minor, Grey Friars or Franciscans, being one of the four orders of mendicant friars,) instituted in 1208. Wadding, an Irishman and a Minorite, who lived in the first half of the seventeenth century, and who wrote a history of his order, expressly refers it to Celano. He mentions two other hymns or Sequences composed by him, one beginning: *Fregit victor virtualis;* the other: *Sanctitatis nova signa.* The circumstance of the Dominican Sixtus Senenfis affecting to sneer at it, calling it *rhythmus inconditus*, is regarded as confirmatory of the opinion, that it was at least the work of a Franciscan; the bitter rivalries subsisting between the two orders affording, it is thought, the most plausible explanation of a criticism so manifestly splenetic and unjust. Another corroborative circumstance is its early admission into the Franciscan Missals, by which means a knowledge of it was spread throughout Europe. The correctness of this inference is further sustained by the fact, that, inscribed on a marble slab in the Franciscan Church of St. Francis at Mantua, was found one of the earliest copies of the hymn, representing, it is believed, the text as it came from the hands of the author. Dr. Mohnike, a learned and able editor of the Dies Iræ, furnishes an old copy of the Mantuan text, which differs from the Received text chiefly in this, that the first four stanzas are additional. They are here given with a translation annexed; also the heading which is as follows :

Meditatio Vetusta et Venusta
   de Novissimo Judicio
quæ Mantuæ in æde D. Francisci in
   marmore legitur.

1. Cogita, anima fidelis,
   Ad quid respondere velis,
   Christo venturo de cœlis.

    Weigh with solemn thought and tender,
    What response, thou, Soul, wilt render,
    Then when Christ shall come in splendor.

2. Cum deposcet rationem
   Ob boni omissionem,
   Ob mali commissionem.

    And thy life shall be inspected,
    All its hidden guilt detected,
    Evil done and good neglected.

3. Dies illa, dies iræ,
   Quam conemur prævenire
   Obviamque Deo ire;

    For that day of vengeance neareth :
    Ready be each one that heareth
    God to meet when He appeareth,

4. Seria contritione,
   Gratiæ apprehenfione,
   Vitæ emendatione.

   By repenting, by believing,
   By God's offered grace receiving,
   By all evil courfes leaving.

The succeeding fixteen verfes are the same, with flight variations, as those of the Church or Received text; but in place of the next verse, which forms the 17th of this, beginning: *Oro supplex et acclinis*, the Mantuan copy has the following for its 21ft and concluding ftanza:

21. Confors ut beatitatis
    Vivam cum juftificatis
    In ævum æternitatis. Amen.

   That in fellowfhip fraternal
   With inhabitants supernal
   I may live the life eternal. Amen.

That the abbreviation of the poem, by the omiffion of the four opening ftanzas, adds greatly to its general, and ftill more to its lyric effectiveness, there can be no doubt. The rejected verfes, partaking of a quiet and meditative character, impair the force of the lyric element. In its present form, all is vehement ſtir and movement, from the grand and ſtartling abruptness of its opening, to the sweet and powerful pathos of its solemn and impreſſive close.

Beſides Celano, various other names have had their supporters for the honor of the authorſhip of this poem. It has been attributed to Gregory the Great, who lived at a period some ſix hundred years earlier. But this would involve the neceſſity of suppoſing that a poem of such extraordinary merit could remain unknown and unnoticed during so many centuries, which is not at all likely. Beſides, it is certain, that, while rhyme was not altogether unknown or unused at that time, it had by no means reached that ſtate of perfection which this poem exhibits.*

Leonard Meiſter, a Swiss writer, claimed that Felix Hämmerlin, (Latinized into Malleolus,) a Church dignitary of Zürich, born in 1389, and who died about 1457, was the author of Dies Iræ, because among Hämmerlin's poems he found a manuscript of this hymn; but the evidence is quite concluſive,

* See Appendix—Origin of Latin Rhyme:

xviii   HISTORY OF THE HYMN.

that the hymn was in exiftence before his time. In the Hämmerlin text, the 16th verse is followed by eight more, probably supplied by Hämmerlin himself. They are here subjoined.

17. Oro supplex a ruinis,
    Cor contritum quafi cinis:
    Gere curam mei finis!

    From the ruins of creation,
    Make I contrite supplication:
    Interpose for my salvation!

18. Lachrymosa die illa,
    Cum resurget ex favilla,
    Tanquam ignis ex scintilla,

    On that day of woe and weeping,
    When, like fire from spark upleaping,
    Starts, from afhes where he's fleeping,

19. Judicandus homo reus,
    Huic ergo parce, Deus!
    Efto semper adjutor meus!

    Man account to Thee to render:
    Spare the miserable offender!
    Be my Helper and Defender!

20. Quando cœli sunt movendi,
    Dies adsunt tunc tremendi,
    Nullum tempus pœnitendi.

    When the heavens away are flying,
    Days of trembling then and crying,
    For repentance time denying;

21. Sed salvatis læta dies,
    Et damnatis nulla quies,
    Sed dæmonum effigies.

    To the saved a day of gladness,
    To the damned a day of sadness,
    Demon forms and shapes of madness.

22. O tu Deus majestatis,
    Alme candor Trinitatis,
    Nunc conjunge cum beatis!

    God of infinite perfection,
    Trinity's serene reflection,
    Give me part with the election!

23. Vitam meam fac felicem
    Propter tuam genetricem,
    Jesse florem et radicem.

Happiness upon me shower,
For Thy Mother's sake, with power
Who is Jesse's root and flower.

24. Præsta nobis tunc levamen,
Dulce nostrum fac certamen,
Ut clamemus omnes, Amen!

From Thy fulness comfort pour us,
Fight Thou with us or fight for us,
So we'll shout, Amen, in chorus.

Taking for granted that the Mantuan was the original text, it would follow that the truncation of the four introductory verses spoken of had already taken place at the time of Hämmerlin; and it is furthermore obvious that the 17th and 18th verses of the Received text must have been formed out of the first three of the supplemented verses of Hämmerlin, as follows, viz. : by substituting, in the 17th verse, " et acclinis " for " a ruinis," and taking the first two lines of the two succeeding verses, being triplets, to make up the 18th verse, which consists of four lines. Bating a few verbal variations, the first sixteen verses of the Hämmerlin and

Church texts correspond. The last named is founded on the Roman Missal first published in 1567, under the sanction and after the revision of the Council of Trent. It forms the basis of the present, as it does of most translations.

A brief reference to some of the more important variations in the text, and an explanation of certain allusions which occur therein, may not be uninteresting. The first line, *Dies iræ, dies illa*, plainly points to a passage of Scripture from the Vulgate,— Zephaniah I. 15. The whole verse reads thus: " DIES IRÆ, DIES ILLA, dies tribulationis et angustiæ, dies calamitatis et miseriæ, dies tenebrarum et caliginis, dies nebulæ et turbinis, dies tubæ et clangoris." In the third line, the change of the Mantuan reading, " Petro " into " David," as it now stands, may have been due, it is conjectured, to a feeling that there was greater appropriateness in David's being associated with the ante-Christian Sibyl. From the aversion felt to the introduction of a heathen Sibyl into a Christian and still more a Church hymn, a Missal of the diocese of Metz, published in 1778, rejecting the third line, adopts, but without the authority of a single manuscript, another reading as follows :

> Dies iræ, dies illa,
> Crucis expandens vexilla,
> Solvet sæclum in favilla.

> Day of wrath, that day amazing,
> High the bannered cross upraising,
> While the universe is blazing.

The allusion here is to the sign of the coming of the Son of Man in heaven, mentioned in Matthew xxiv. 3 ; and is indicative of the belief, that the sign there spoken of would have its fulfilment in the apparition of a cross in the sky. But the older and the true reading is doubtless the other, which refers to the Sibyl as bearing concurrent testimony with the prophet of the Old or the New Testament, David or Peter, (Psalm xcvi. 13 ; xcvii. 3 ; xi. 6 ; 2 Peter iii. 7,) touching the destruction of the world and the final judgment. The 2d, 7th, and 8th books of the "Sibylline Oracles" are full of passages which refer to these, but it is probable that the reference here is more immediately to verses extracted therefrom, found in Lactantius (Divin. Institut. lib. vii. De Vita Beata, cap. 16–24). In the earlier ages of the Church, these pretended prophecies were regarded with no little veneration; wherefore it is by no means uncommon to find Christian writers placing them side by side with Scriptural prophecies, and, as in the case before us, making solemn appeal to them. The discovery of their true character as worthless forgeries was reserved for a later period.

This poem, which, there is every reason to believe, was originally the inspiration of retirement, the solitary outpouring of

> "a suppliant heart all crushed
> And crumbled into contrite dust,"—

to adopt the language of Crashaw's version at the 17th verse,—came afterwards, when it had passed into Church use, to receive the title of SEQUENCE, from the place assigned to it in the service of the Mass for the Dead. The precise time when this occurred cannot be determined, but it must have been early, for Albizzi speaks of it as being in common use as a Sequence in 1385. For an explanation of this term, the reader is referred to the Appendix at the end of this volume.

If the origin of the hymn be somewhat obscure, not so have been its subsequent fortunes. Through the long centuries that have elapsed since the time it first became known to the world, its extraordinary merits have been steadily recognized. Its light has been that of a star, whose keen and diamond lustre intermits not nor grows dim, but shines on the same from age to age. Its mission from the beginning has been one of power. To some, there is reason to believe, it has been "the power of God unto salvation." Scattered everywhere along its track are seen the luminous footprints of its victorious progress as the subduer of hearts. The greatest minds have delighted to bear testimony to its worth. Goethe evinced his appreciation of it by introducing certain verses of it into his "Fauft,"—with how grand an effect we all know. Boswell relates of Dr. Johnson, that, "when he would try to repeat the celebrated *Prosa Ecclesiastica pro Mortuis*, beginning : *Dies iræ, dies illa*, he could never pass the stanza ending thus : *Tantus labor non sit cassus*, without bursting into a flood of tears."

It is said that Ancina, a Profeſſor of Medicine in the Univerſity of Turin, was so ſtrongly affected by hearing one day the Dies Iræ chanted in the service for the dead, that he determined to abandon the world. He afterwards became Biſhop of Saluzzo. Milman, in his "Hiſtory of Chriſtianity," speaking of the Latin poetry of the Chriſtian Church, remarks: "There is nothing, in my judgment, to be compared with the monkiſh *Dies iræ, dies illa.*" To these names might be added those of many other eminent scholars and critics, all bearing like teſtimony. But the crowning proof of its unrivalled excellence is found in the fact, that, mingled with the ſighs and gaspings of diſſolving Nature, the measured beat of its melodious rhythm has been so often heard; now, it may be, in the soft murmur of words half audible, and now in the clear tones of a diſtinct utterance, iſſuing from the pale and trembling lips of the dying. The Earl of Roscommon, we are told, repeated with great energy and devotion, in the moment when he expired, two lines of his own tranſlation of the 17th verse :—

> "My God, my Father, and my Friend,
> Do not forsake me in my end!"

Sir Walter Scott evinced his regard for it in the same affecting manner, during his laſt hours: "We very often," says his biographer, "heard diſtinctly the cadence of the Dies Iræ."

It is certainly somewhat remarkable, that, while thus solemnly aſſociated with the dying moments of these two illuſtrious maſters of song, who had likewise employed their pens in the taſk of rendering it into Engliſh, it ſhould have had a connection not diſſimilar with the death of that great composer by whose means this immortal poem has come to be worthily wedded to immortal muſic. It is well known that Mozart's Requiem is founded on it. This, his greateſt work, perhaps, was deſtined also to be his laſt, of which, it is said, he had a solemn presentiment. His death occurred before it was entirely finiſhed. Beſides Mozart, other diſtinguiſhed composers, such as Cherubini, Haydn, Jomelli, Paläſtrina, and Pergoleſi, have exercised their genius upon the same theme and the same text.

TRANSLATIONS OF THE HYMN.

HE number of translations made of this hymn into different languages it were not easy to estimate. Those in German are particularly numerous. In a work dedicated to these, edited by Dr. F. G. Lisco, (Berlin, 1840,) as many as seventy versions, more or less complete, are given; the number being further increased three years afterwards by the addition of seventeen others, appended to a volume of translations, by the same editor, of the Stabat Mater.*

---

* For the loan of both the above works the writer is indebted to the Rev. William R. Williams, D. D., who, in a Note, afterwards somewhat enlarged and thrown into an Appendix, affixed to an Address on the " Conservative Principle of our Literature," first published in 1843, and subsequently included in his volume of " Miscellanies," has, with his usual

xxviii TRANSLATIONS OF THE HYMN.

There is one in French, one in Romaic or Modern Greek, one in Dutch, and one in Latin, all the reſt being German. In nearly every case, pains have been taken to preserve the exact measure and form of the original. The superior flexibility of the German, and its greater supply of words adapted for double rhyme, give tranſlators in that language a decided advantage. The difficulty involved in triplicating the double rhymes, owing to the poverty of our language in words suitable for the purpose, without practiſing awkward and inelegant inverſions, is probably the reason why English tranſlators, even where they have been careful to retain the triplet form of the ſtanza, have failed to preserve the rhyming close.

Craſhaw's, one of the oldeſt and nobleſt of the English tranſlations, and which in the opinion of an eminent critic was not surpaſſed by anything he ever wrote, is done in quatrains, or ſingle rhymed couplets

eloquence and exhauſtive learning, given a very full and inſtructive account of this hymn and its tranſlations; adding in the later editions a verſion of his own, one of the first made in ternary double rhyme.

repeated; and, on account of the freeness of the rendering, might more properly be called a reproduction than a tranflation. The Earl of Roscommon, celebrated in Dryden's verse as the greateft poet of his time, was the author of a verfion praised by Pope as the beft of his poetical performances; although he is confidered as having borrowed both from Crafhaw and Dryden. It is in triplets like the original, but without double rhyme, and the verse is iambic inftead of trochaic.

The few verfes introduced by Sir Walter Scott into the "Lay of the Laft Minftrel," and which have found their way into almoft all the more recent Collections of Hymns used in our Churches, though spirited and impreffive, can scarcely be called a translation, being little more than an echo of one or two of the leading sentiments of the Latin original. Another familiar hymn, contained in moft Hymn books, commencing,

"Lo! He comes in clouds descending,"

purports to be a tranflation of the Dies Iræ; but in respect neither to form nor spirit does it correspond very accurately to the original. Although there are other verſions of more or less merit, some made by our own scholars, a further enumeration might be tedious. "It is not wonderful," as Trench remarks, "that a poem such as this ſhould have continually allured and continually defied tranſlators."

The Author of the Tranſlations here publiſhed scarcely knows how to ſhield himself from the imputation of presumption to which his attempt exposes him. The number of his verſions is Thirteen. The first ſix have the somewhat rare merit, so far at leaſt as Engliſh verſions are concerned, of being metrically conformed, both as it respects rhyme and rhythm, to the original. The five succeeding ones are like in rhythm, but vary from the original in not preserving the double rhyme. The one which follows is in iambic triplets, like Roscommon's; and the laſt in quatrains, after the manner of Craſhaw's verſion.

It has been the aim of the Tranſlator to be in all caſes as faithful as poſſible to the senſe and spirit of the original, and likewise to the letter, but not ſo ſlaviſhly as to preclude variety. He has endeavored to carry out likeness in unlikeness, and to give to each verſion, so far as practicable, the intereſt of a diſtinct poem. How far he has succeeded others muſt judge. The preservation of the double rhyme involved some special difficulties, which he has overcome as well as he could ; but he would not be surprised if some readers preferred the eaſier metres, and indulges the hope that the multiplication of verſions may serve, among other things, to meet this diverſity of taſte. But there are some, if he mistakes not, who enjoy those pleasing surprises in viewing an object, that result from an altered attitude and a new angle of vision,—the curious changes which follow every fresh turn of a revolving kaleidoscope,—and the writer is willing therefore to believe that such, at any rate, will not be displeased at this attempt to supply the deficiency of one verſion by another and yet another, in the hope that thereby the original may be exhibited, approximately at least, in its solid entireness.

Young, in his "Eſſay on Lyric Poetry," aſſerts that difficulty overcome gives grace and pleasure, and he accounts for the pleasure of rhyme in general upon this principle. Having failed in his own case to afford an exemplification of great success in this particular, his critic and biographer, Johnson, somewhat sarcastically remarks: "But then the writer must take care that the difficulty is overcome; that is, he must make rhyme consist with as perfect sense and expression as would be expected, if he were perfectly free from that shackle." Hence, the greater the difficulties to be surmounted, the greater is the need of elaboration, until art conceals art.

The present Translator, recognizing fully the propriety of the rule here stated, does not feel that he has any right to plead the arduousness of his task, as an excuse for any instances, if such there be, of forced and unnatural construction, resorted to in order to meet the exigencies of rhyme or metre. What is called poetic license is, he is aware, a license of power and grace, and not of weakness and deformity, being tantamount to a license to dance or sing, in place of ordinary walking or speaking. Poetic chains, undoubtedly, were meant not to confine and cripple, but to regulate movement in conformity with settled laws; the object being, not to punish speech, but to exalt and honor it,—to grace language, not disgrace it.

To preserve, in connection with the utmost fidelity and strictness of rendering, all the rhythmic merits of the Latin original,—to attain to a vital likeness as well as to an exact literalness, at the same time that nothing is sacrificed of its musical sonorousness and billowy grandeur, easy and graceful in its swing as the ocean on its bed,—to make the verbal copy, otherwise cold and dead, glow with the fire of lyric passion,—to reflect, and that too by means of a single version, the manifold aspects of the many-sided original, exhausting at once its wonderful fulness and pregnancy,—to cause the white light of the primitive so to pass through the medium of another language as that it shall undergo no refraction whatever,—would be desirable, certainly, were it practicable; but so much as this it were unreasonable to expect in any translation.

All the versions here given were written and nearly ready for the press more than two years ago; but, influenced partly by a sense of their imperfectness, and partly by a doubt as to the reception that a book exclusively devoted to a single hymn might meet with from the public, the Translator has delayed their appearance until now, when, encouraged by the favorable opinion expressed by some, whose names, were it proper to give them, would be regarded, he doubts not, as an apology for his boldness, he ventures the experiment of publication. He does not deny that the amount of public favor that has been already accorded to two of the versions, viz., those marked I. and II., published anonymously in the "Newark Daily Advertiser" several years since, the first as long ago as 1847, has had something to do with overcoming his distrust. To avoid misapprehension, it is right to state, that two verses of the first were introduced into Mrs. Stowe's "Uncle Tom's Cabin," and by these accidental means have enjoyed a world-wide currency. More recently this version has been honored with a place in the "Plymouth Collection of Hymns and Tunes," edited by Henry Ward Beecher, and set to music. It was, so far as the Translator knows, the first attempt, with a single exception, to reproduce in English the ternary double rhyme of the original.

ET STATUET OVES QUIDEM A DEXTRIS SUIS, HÆDOS AUTEM A SINISTRIS.
St. Math. Ch. XXV.

DE NOVISSIMO JUDICIO.

IES iræ, dies illa
Solvet sæclum in favillâ,
Teste David cum Sibyllâ.

Quantus tremor est futurus,
Quando Judex est venturus,
Cuncta strictè discussurus!

Tuba, mirum spargens sonum
Per sepulchra regionum,
Coget omnes ante thronum.

Mors stupebit et natura,
Quum resurget creatura
Judicanti responsura.

Liber scriptus proferetur,
In quo totum continetur,
De quo mundus judicetur.

Judex ergo quum sedebit,
Quidquid latet, apparebit,
Nil inultum remanebit.

Quod sum miser tunc dicturus,
Quem patronum rogaturus,
Quum vix justus sit securus?

Rex tremendæ majestatis,
Qui salvandos salvas gratis,
Salva me, fons pietatis!

Recordare, Jesu pie,
Quod sum causa tuæ viæ,
Ne me perdas illâ die!

Quærens me sedisti lassus,
Redemisti crucem passus:
Tantus labor non sit cassus!

DIES IRÆ.

Juste Judex ultionis,
Donum fac remissionis
Ante diem rationis!

Ingemisco tanquam reus,
Culpâ rubet vultus meus:
Supplicanti parce, Deus!

Qui Mariam absolvisti,
Et latronem exaudisti,
Mihi quoque spem dedisti.

Præces meæ non sunt dignæ,
Sed tu bonus fac benignè
Ne perenni cremer igne!

Inter oves locum præsta,
Et ab hædis me sequestra,
Statuens in parte dextrâ!

Confutatis maledictis,
Flammis acribus addictis,
Voca me cum benedictis!

Oro supplex et acclinis,
Cor contritum quasi cinis:
Gere curam mei finis!

Lachrymosa dies illa,
Qua resurget ex favillâ,
Judicandus homo reus :
Huic ergo parce, Deus!

I.

AY of wrath, that day of burning,
Seer and Sibyl speak concerning,
All the world to ashes turning.

Oh, what fear shall it engender,
When the Judge shall come in splendor,
Strict to mark and just to render!

Trumpet, scattering sounds of wonder,
Rending sepulchres asunder,
Shall resistless summons thunder.

All aghast then Death shall shiver,
And great Nature's frame shall quiver,
When the graves their dead deliver.

Book, where actions are recorded,
All the ages have afforded,
Shall be brought and dooms awarded.

When shall sit the Judge unerring,
He'll unfold all here occurring,
No just vengeance then deferring.

What shall *I* say, that time pending?
Ask what advocate's befriending,
When the just man needs defending?

Dreadful King, all power possessing,
Saving freely those confessing,
Save thou me, O Fount of Blessing!

Think, O Jesus, for what reason
Thou didst bear earth's spite and treason,
Nor me lose in that dread season!

Seeking me Thy worn feet hasted,
On the cross Thy soul death tasted:
Let such travail not be wasted!

DIES IRÆ.

Righteous Judge of retribution!
Make me gift of absolution
Ere that day of execution!

Culprit-like, I plead, heart-broken,
On my cheek shame's crimson token:
Let the pardoning word be spoken!

Thou, who Mary gav'st remission,
Heard'st the dying Thief's petition,
Cheer'st with hope my lost condition.

Though my prayers be void of merit,
What is needful, Thou confer it,
Lest I endless fire inherit!

Be there, Lord, my place decided
With Thy sheep, from goats divided,
Kindly to Thy right hand guided!

When th' accursed away are driven,
To eternal burnings given,
Call me with the blessed to heaven!

I beseech Thee, proſtrate lying,
Heart as aſhes, contrite, ſighing,
Care for me when I am dying!

Day of tears and late repentance,
Man ſhall rise to hear his sentence:
Him, the child of guilt and error,
Spare, Lord, in that hour of terror!

II.

AY shall dawn that has no morrow,
Day of vengeance, day of sorrow,
As from Prophecy we borrow.

It shall burn, that day of trouble,
As a furnace heated double,
And the wicked shall be stubble.

O, what trembling, when the rifted
Skies shall show the Judge uplifted,
And all strictly shall be sifted!

Trump shall sound a blast appalling,
On the grave's deep stillness falling,
Small and great before Him calling.

Death with fear shall be o'ertaken,
Nature to her base be shaken,
When the sleeping dead shall waken.

Volume shall be brought, whose pages
Register the deeds of ages,
Whence the world shall have just wages.

When that Court shall hold its session,
Every mouth shall make confession,
Left unpunished no transgression.

How, alas! in that dread season,
Shall I answer for my treason,
When the righteous fear with reason?

Awful King, who nothing cravest,
Since Thyself full ransom gavest,
Save Thou me, who freely savest!

Me, for whom, with love so tender,
Thou didst leave Thy throne of splendor,
Jesus, do not then surrender!

Wearily for me Thou toiledst,
Diedst for me and Satan spoiledst:
Let not triumph whom Thou foiledst!

Thou, whose frown will be damnation,
Grant me earnest of salvation,
Ere that day of consummation!

Culprit-like, I, self-convicted,
Blushing, prostrate, and afflicted,
Kneel for mercy unrestricted.

Thou, who Mary's faith rewardedst,
Pardon to the Thief accordedst,
Me, too, trembling hope affordedst.

Poor my prayers, but give ensample
Of Thy goodness rich and ample,
Lest insulted Justice trample!

With Thy chosen flock unspotted,
Severed from the herd besotted,
Be my place that day allotted!

When Thy curse shall blast and wither,
Doom to hell and banish thither,
Bid me with the blessed, Come hither!

Care for me as one who feareth,
One who hasteth when he heareth,
When my solemn exit neareth!

When the light of that day flashes,
And man rises from his ashes
At Thy bar account to render,
Spare then, Lord, the pale offender!

III.

AY of Vengeance and of Wages,
Fiery goal of all the ages,
Burden of prophetic pages!

Guilty wretches, vainly fleeing
From that flaming Eye, whose seeing
Searches all the depths of being.

Wakened by that Trump of Wonder,
Answering Earthquakes, roaring under,
Heave and split the ground asunder;

And the buried generations,
People of all times and nations,
Live again and take their stations,

Each immortal pale offender,
Round the Great White Throne of Splendor,
Strict account to God to render;

Who, unmocked and unmistaken,
Shall pronounce the doom unshaken,
And long slumbering vengeance waken.

What if weighed and found deficient?
Standing at that bar omniscient,
Who hath righteousness sufficient?

King of Holiness unspotted,
By Thy merit me allotted
Let my guilt be freely blotted!

Me, for whom Thou shame didst borrow,
Trod'st the paths of earthly sorrow,
Lose not on that dreadful morrow!

Seeking me Thou weary sankest,
All my cup of trembling drankest,
Nor from death, to save me, shrankest.

Must I sink yet to perdition?
God of Vengeance, grant remission,
Ere that Day of Inquisition!

Filled with shame and consternation,
Lifting hands of supplication,
Spare me, God of my Salvation!

Let such grace be manifested,
As on weeping Mary rested,
As was towards the Thief attested!

Though no worth in me discerning,
Spurn not, though I merit spurning:
Rescue me from endless burning!

When division is effected
'Mong the race of men collected,
Leave me not with the rejected!

When Thy curse from Thee shall sever,
Kindling hells, extinguished never,
Join me to Thyself forever!

From the ashes of contrition,
From the depths I make petition:
Grant my soul a safe dismission!

When that day ſhall snare th' unwary,
And ſhall guilty man unbury,
Spare me then, Dread Adversary!

IV.

AY of Prophecy! it flashes,
Falling spheres together dashes,
And the world consumes to ashes.

O, what fear of wrath impending,
When the Judge is seen descending,
Inquisition strict intending!

God's awakening Trump shall scatter
Summons through the world of matter,
And the Throne of Death shall shatter.

What amazement, when forgotten
Generations, dead and rotten,
Suddenly are rebegotten!

Book and Record universal
Shall be opened for rehearsal,
Whence the doom without reversal.

When by that dread Judge inspected,
Nothing shall pass undetected,
Unavenged nor uncorrected.

How shall I, a wretch unstable,
Bide that hour inevitable,
When the just man scarce is able?

Dreadful King, from Thee, the Giver,
Flows salvation like a river:
Fount of Mercy, me deliver!

Thou, who, touched with my condition,
Sought to save me from perdition,
Be Thou mindful of Thy mission!

Let Thy death for my offences,
Horror of Thy soul and senses,
Be not void of consequences!

Blot my sins, ere that revision,
Day of ultimate decision,
When Thy foes are in derision!

From my eyes repentance gushes,
O'er my cheeks spread crimson blushes:
Spare the worm Thy terror crushes!

Thou, who wert of old most gracious
Ev'n to sinners most audacious,
Is Thy mercy now less spacious?

Worthless all the prayers I offer:
Grace must seal what grace doth proffer,
Else I perish with the scoffer.

When Thou makest separation,
With Thy sheep assign my station,
Saints of every age and nation!

When the malison eternal
Banishes to fires infernal,
Bid me enter realms supernal!

Thou, who dost, with care unsleeping,
Keep that trusted to Thy keeping,
Save my eyes from endless weeping!

Day of tears, consuming, cruel,
With a burning world for fuel,
Man shall rise from glowing embers,
Made complete in all his members:
Ah! what plea will then be valid,
When the sinner, trembling, pallid,
Waits to hear his sentence given?
Spare him then, O God of Heaven!

V.

AY of vengeance, end of scorning,
World in afhes, world in mourning,
Whereof Prophets utter warning!

O, what trembling, when the falling
Rocks and mountains hear men calling,
"Hide me from that face appalling!"

Freezing fear the blood will thicken,
Death and Hell be horror-ftricken,
When the myftic Trump fhall quicken

All the buried duft of ages,—
Monarchs, chieftains, ftatesmen, sages,
Actors on unnumbered ftages,—

Summoned to the dread recital
Of that Record ftrict and vital,
Basis of a juft requital.

Every mafk of falsehood riven, —
Guilt, from every covert driven,
Shall to punifhment be given.

'Mid the horror and confufion
Of that sorrowful conclufion
Of each miserable delufion,

Whither, ah! fhall I betake me?
Thou, O King, whose terrors fhake me,
Of Thy grace a trophy make me!

Jesus! by Thine incarnation,
By Thy miffion of salvation,
Then avert juft condemnation!

By Thy pity, love unfailing,
By the cross's bitter nailing,
Let not all be unavailing!

Dread Avenger of transgreffion,
Cleanse these lips that make confeffion,
Ere th' awards of that laft seffion.

Spare a culprit, groans fast heaving,
Self-convicted, blushing, grieving,
In Thy power and grace believing.

Since Thy nature doth not vary,
Thou, who heard'st the Thief and Mary,
My transgressions blot and bury!

Worthless works behind me casting—
Grace must save, not prayer nor fasting,
From the fire that's everlasting.

On Thy right hand fix my station
With the chosen generation,
In the sheep-fold of salvation!

When Thy curse the wicked chases,
With the blest in heavenly places
Call me to Thy dear embraces!

Care for me, whom guilt abashes,
Prostrate, contrite, heart as ashes,
When that day of terror flashes!

Day of weeping and of wailing,
Human hearts and fates unveiling :
Then, when Time shall be no longer,
And the strong yields to the Stronger,
Death and Hell their dead surrender,
And the Sea its own shall tender,
Multitudinous, unbounded
Generations rise astounded,
Each to answer for his sinning,
He who lived at the beginning,
He who when the world is hoary,—
Spare, O, spare, Thou God of Glory!

VI.

AY of wrath and confternation,
Day of fiery confummation,
Prophefied in Revelation!

O, what horror on all faces,
When the coming Judge each traces,
Flaming, dreadful, in all places!

Trump fhall found, and every fingle
Mortal slumberer's ears fhall tingle,
And the dead fhall rise and mingle:

All of every tribe and nation,
That have lived fince the creation,
Answering that dread citation.

Volume, from which nothing's blotted,
Evil done nor evil plotted,
Shall be brought and dooms allotted.

Judge, who sits at that assizes,
Shall, deceived by no disguises,
Try each work that man devises.

How shall I, a wretch polluted,
Answer then to sins imputed,
When the just man's case is mooted?

Awful Monarch of Creation!
Saving without compensation,
Save me, Fountain of Salvation!

Lose me not then, Jesus, seeing
I am Thine by gift of being,
Doubly Thine by price of freeing!

Thou, the Lord of Life and Glory,
Hung'st a victim gashed and gory:
Let not all be nugatory!

Pardon, Thou whose vengeance smiteth,
But whom mercy most delighteth,
Ere that reck'ning day affrighteth!

As a culprit, stand I groaning,
Blushing, my demerit owning:
Sprinkle me with blood atoning!

Thou, who Mary's sins remittedst,
And the softened Thief acquittedst,
Likewise hope to me permittedst.

Weak these prayers Thy throne assailing;
But let grace, o'er guilt prevailing,
Save me from eternal wailing!

While the goats afar are driven,
'Mid Thy sheep me place be given,
Blood-washed favorites of Heaven!

While "Depart!" shall doom and gather
Those to flame, address me rather:
"Come thou blessed of my Father!"

In my final hour, when faileth
Heart and flesh, and my cheek paleth,
Grant that succor which availeth!

Day unutterably solemn:
Crypt and pyramid and column,
Isle and continent and ocean,
Rocking with a fearful motion,
Shall give up, a countless number
Starting from their long, long slumber,
Horror stamping every feature,
While is judged each sinful creature,
End of pending controversy:
Spare Thou then, O God of Mercy!

VII.

AY of wrath, that day of days,
Present to my thought always,
When the world shall burn and blaze!

O, what trembling, O, what fear,
When th' Omniscient Judge draws near,
Scanning all with eyes severe!

When the Trump of God shall sound
Through the vague and vast profound
Of the regions under ground;

And th' innumerable dead,
Answering to that summons dread,
Shall forsake their dusty bed;

And that Book of ancient date
Shall be opened, whereon wait
Mighty issues big with fate;

And each secret thing shall lie
Thenceforth bare to every eye,
Nought unpunished or passed by.

Ah, me! what shall I then plead,
Who for me then intercede,
When the just of help have need?

Thou, who doft, O Heavenly King,
Free forgiveness freely bring,
Let me drink of Mercy's Spring!

Thou didst empty and exhaust
Heaven for me: when such the cost,
Jesus, let me not be lost!

Wearily Thou soughtest me,
Bought'st me on th' accursèd tree:
Let it not all fruitless be!

Righteous Judge, who wilt repay,
Grant me pardon, ere that day
Of decision and dismay!

I, a sinful man and base,
Blushing, groaning o'er my case,
Seek and supplicate Thy grace.

Thou, who heardest Mary's sighs,
Thou, who openedst Paradise
To the Thief, regard my cries!

Worthless are my prayers and worse,
But, good Lord, be not adverse,
Lest I sink beneath the curse!

Set me, when at Thy command
All mankind divided stand,
With the sheep at Thy right hand!

When th' insufferable doom
Shall the reprobate consume,
With Thy chosen give me room!

In the solemn hour of death,
When the earthly vanisheth,
O, receive my parting breath!

Ah! that day made up of tears,
When from ashes reappears
Th' Adam of six thousand years,—

Who, by its red glare and gleam,
Sees, as in an awful dream,
Justice lift her trembling beam,—

Conscious on that hinge of fate
All things hang and hesitate:
Spare then, Lord, if not too late!

VIII.

THAT dreadful day, my soul!
Which the ages shall unroll,
When the knell of Time shall
toll!

O, the terror and the shame,
When the Judge with eyes of flame
Shall make piercing search of blame!

Suddenly the Trumpet's shock
Doors of Hades shall unlock,
And before Him all shall flock.

Struck with wonder and dismay,
Death and Nature shall obey
Summons to give up their prey.

Loudly each indictment dread
Shall in every ear be read
Of the living and the dead.

Every idle word and thought,
Every work in secret wrought,
Into Judgment shall be brought.

Scarce the just man's case is sure,
Scarce the heavens themselves are pure:
Ah! how then shall I endure?

Dreadful Potentate and high,
Who dost freely justify,
Fount of Grace, my need supply!

Jesus, mind the kind intent
Of Thy weary banishment,
And my ruin then prevent!

Let Thy passion and Thy pain,
All Thou sufferedst me to gain,
Be not barren and in vain!

Righteous Arbiter of fate!
Life and death upon Thee wait,
Pardon, ere it be too late!

Spare me, vilest of the race,
Guilty, infamous and base,
Blushing mendicant of grace!

Though of sinners I be chief,
Hear me, Thou who heard'st the Thief,
Driedst the fount of Mary's grief!

All my prayers are guilty breath,
And the best nought meriteth:
But in mercy save from death!

When, disposed on either hand,
All mankind before Thee stand,
Set me with Thy chosen band!

When, O, terrible to tell!
Yawns inevitable Hell,
With the blessed bid me dwell!

When I reach the awful goal,
And Death's billows o'er me roll,
Care for my undying soul!

Day of weeping and surprise,
Opening tombs and opening eyes,
Rocking earth and burning skies!

Day of universal dread,
When the quick and quickened dead
Shall have solemn sentence said!

Then, O, then, when in despair,
Man shall speak or shriek the prayer,
" Spare me!" God of Mercy, spare!

IX.

AY foretold, that day of ire,
Burden erſt of David's lyre,
When the world ſhall ſink in
fire!

O, what horror and amaze,
When at once on mortal gaze
All the Judge's pomp ſhall blaze!

When the Trumpet's myſtic blaſt,
To the world's four corners caſt,
Disentombs the buried Paſt;

And from all the heaving sod,
From each foot of trampled clod,
Starts a multitude to God;

And that Volume is unrolled
Wherein are minutely told
All men's doings from of old;

While, from what is there contained,
Shall be judged a world arraigned,
And eternal fates ordained:

What defence can I then make,
To what Patron me betake,
When the righteous fear and quake?

King, who doft all power poffess,
Free Thy grace and limitless,
Save me, Fount of Bleffedness!

Jefus, Mafter, Thou doft know
I Thy miffion caused below,
All Thy weariness and woe!

Let Thy blood, that drenched the hilt
Of that sword unfheathed for guilt,
Be not vainly fhed and spilt!

O my Judge, forgive, forget!
Cancel my tremendous debt,
Ere the sun of grace fhall set!

Filled with shame I hang my head,
Blushes deep my face o'erspread:
Stay Thy lightnings fierce and red!

Thou canst darkest stains efface;
Hast made monuments of grace
Of the vilest of the race.

My poor prayers please not repel!
Grace and goodness with Thee dwell:
Snatch me from the flames of Hell!

When Thou shalt discriminate,
Sheep from goats shalt separate,
Let me on Thy right hand wait!

When Thy sentence, smiting dumb,
Down to Hell shall banish some,
With the blessed bid me come!

To Thy care, O Kind as Just!
Heart all penitential dust,
I my end commit and trust!

Floods of tears that day shall pour;
Man shall wake to sleep no more;
Guilty, horribly afraid :
Spare him, Lord, whom Thou hast made!

X.

O! it comes, with stealthy feet,
Day, the ages shall complete,
When the world shall melt with heat!

O, what trembling shall there be,
When all eyes the Judge shall see,
Come to sift iniquity!

Trump shall syllable command,
And the dead of sea and land
All before the Throne shall stand.

Death shall shudder, Nature too,
When the creature lives anew,
Called to render answer true.

Volume, that omitteth nought
Man e'er said or did or thought,
Shall for sentence then be brought.

When shall sit the Judge severe,
All that's dark shall be made clear,
Nothing unavenged appear.

What, alas! shall I then say,
To what Intercessor pray,
When the just shrink with dismay?

Awful King, since all is free,
Without merit, without fee,
Fount of Mercy, save Thou me!

Mind, O Jesus, Friend sincere,
How I caused Thy advent here,
Nor me lose who cost so dear!

Straying, I by Thee was sought,
On the cross with blood was bought:
Let it not be all for nought!

Righteous Judge! Avenging Lord!
Full remission me afford,
Ere that final day's award!

Groan I, like a culprit base,
Conscious guilt inflames my face:
Spare the suppliant, God of Grace!

Thou, who erſt didſt Mary clear,
And the dying Thief didſt hear,
Hope haſt given me to cheer.

Though my prayers create no claim,
Be propitious, Lord, the same,
Leſt I burn in endless flame!

Place among Thy ſheep provide,
From the goats me sunder wide,
Standing safe at Thy right ſide!

While "Depart!" to foes addreſſed
Baniſheth to woes ungueſſed,
Call me near Thee with the bleſſed!

Contrite pangs my bosom tear,
Heart as aſhes: hear my prayer,
Let my end be not despair!

On that day of grief and dread,
When man, rifing from the dead,
Shall eternal juftice face,
Spare the finner, God of Grace!

XI.

AY of wrath, that day of dole,
When a fire shall wrap the whole,
And the earth be burnt to coal!

O, what horror, smiting dumb
When the Judge of all shall come,
Sinful deeds to search and sum!

Trump's reverberating roar
Through the sepulchres shall pour,
Citing all the Throne before.

Death and Nature stand aghast,
While the dead in numbers vast
Rise to answer for the past.

Volume, writ by God's own pen,
Chronicling the deeds of men,
Shall be brought, and dooms be then.

When the Judge shall sit, behold!
What is secret He'll unfold,
No juſt puniſhment withhold.

Ah! what plea ſhall I prepare,
To what Patron make my prayer,
When the juſt well-nigh despair?

King, majeſtic beyond thought,
Whose free grace cannot be bought,
Save me, whose desert is nought!

O, remember, Jeſus, I
Was the cause and reason why
Thou didſt come on earth to die!

Me Thou sought'ſt with weary feet,
And my ransom didſt complete:
Let such pity nought defeat!

Judge, inflexible and ſtrict,
Pardon, ere that day convict
And th' unchanging doom inflict!

Like a criminal I sigh,
Blushing, penitently cry:
Pass, Lord, my offences by!

Thou, who Mary erst did'st bless,
Heard'st the Thief in his distress,
Hope hast given me no less.

Worthless are my prayers and vain,
But in love do not disdain,
Lest I reap eternal pain!

On Thy right hand grant me place
'Mid the sheep, a chosen race,—
Far from goats devoid of grace!

When the thunder of Thine ire
Headlong hurls to quenchless fire,
Let Thy welcome me inspire!

I entreat Thee, bending low,
Heart as ashes, full of woe,
Succor in my end bestow!

When upon that day of tears
Man from duſt again appears,
Fate depending on Thy nod:
Spare the ſinner then, O God!

XII.

DAY of wrath! O day of fate!
Day foreordained and ultimate,
When all things here shall terminate!

What numbers horribly afraid,
When comes the Judge, in fear arrayed,
To try the creatures He hath made!

The blare of Trumpet, pealing clear,
Shall through the sepulchres career,
And wake the dead, and bring them near.

Astonished Nature then shall quail,
What time the yawning graves unveil,
And man comes forth, amazed and pale,

To answer: The o'erwritten scroll
Shall charge and certify the whole,
Whence shall be judged each human soul.

The Judge enthroned shall bring to light
Whate'er is hid, in open sight
Avenge and vindicate the right.

Ah! with what plea shall I then come,
When, terror-locked, each sense is numb,
And even righteous lips are dumb?

O King immortal and supreme,
Whose fear is great, whose grace extreme,
Make me to drink of Mercy's stream!

Remember, Jesus, Thou didst make
Thyself incarnate for my sake,
Left Hell insatiate claim and take!

Thou soughtest me when far astray,
Didst on the cross my ransom pay:
Let not such love be thrown away!

Just Judge, of purity intense,
Remit my infinite offence,
Before that day of recompense!

Like one convinced of heinous deed,
I groan, I weep, I blush, I plead:
Lord, spare me in that hour of need!

Thou, who wert moved by Mary's tears,
Absolved the Robber from his fears,
Hast given me hope in former years.

My prayers are worthless well I know;
But, good, do Thou Thy goodness show,
And save me from impending woe!

Number and place me 'mong Thy own,
Beneath the shelter of Thy Throne,
Until Thy wrath be overblown!

When that the almighty word shall leap
From out Thy Throne, Thy foes to sweep,
My soul in perfect safety keep!

In prostrate worship, I implore,
With heart all penitent and sore:
Then care for me when life is o'er!

Ah! on that day of grief and dread,
And resurrection of the dead,
Of trial and of just award,
In wrath remember mercy, Lord!

XIII.

HAT day, that awful day, the laſt,
Result and sum of all the Paſt,
Great neceſſary day of doom,
When wrecking fires ſhall all consume!

What dreadful ſhrieks the air ſhall rend,
When all ſhall see the Judge descend,
And hear th' Archangel's echoing ſhout
From heavenly spaces ringing out!

The Trump of God with quickening breath
Shall pierce the ſilent realms of Death,
And sound the summons in each ear:
"Arise! thy Maker calls! Appear!"

From eaſt to weſt, from south to north,
The earth ſhall travail and bring forth;

As desert's sands and ocean's waves
Shall be the sum of empty graves.

Th' unchanging Record of the Paſt
Shall then be read from firſt to laſt;
And out of things therein contained,
Shall all be judged and fates ordained.

No lying tongue, that truth diſtorts,
Shall witness in that Court of Courts;
Each secret thing ſhall be revealed,
And every righteous sentence sealed.

Ah! who can ſtand when He appears?
Confront the guilt of ſinful years?
What hope for me, a wretch depraved,
When scarce the righteous man is saved?

Dread Monarch of the Earth and Heaven!
For that salvation's great 'tis given;
And ſince the boon is wholly free,
O Fount of Pity, save Thou me!

Remember, Jesus, how my case
Once moved Thy pity and Thy grace,
And brought Thee down on earth to stay:
O, lose me not, then, on that day!

I seek Thee, who didst seek me first,
Weary and hungry and athirst;
Didst pay my ransom on the tree:
Let not such travail frustrate be!

Just Judge of vengeance in the end,
Now in the accepted time befriend!
My sins, O, graciously remit,
Ere Thou judicially shalt sit!

Low at Thy feet I groaning lie;
With blushing cheek, and weeping eye,
And stammering lips, I urge the prayer:
O spare me, God of Mercy, spare!

When Mary Thy forgiveness sought,
Wept, but articulated nought,

Thou didſt forgive; didſt hear the brief
Petition of the dying Thief.

On grace thus great my hope is built
That Thou wilt cancel, too, my guilt;
That, though my prayers are worthless breath,
Thou wilt deliver me from death.

When Thy dividing rod of might
Appointeth ſtations oppoſite,
Among Thy ſheep grant me to ſtand,
Far from the goats, at Thy right hand!

And when despair ſhall seize each heart
That hears the dreadful sound, "Depart!"
Be mine, the heavenly lot of some,
To hear that word of welcome, "Come!"

I come to Thee with trembling truſt,
And lay my forehead in the duſt;
In my laſt hour do Thou befriend,
And glorify Thee in my end!

APPENDIX.—SEQUENCE.

A STATEMENT of the order observed in the celebration of Mass will beſt explain the nature and import of this term, in its application by the Romiſh Church to a large body of hymns,—Daniel, in the 5th volume of his learned and laborious work, "Thesaurus Hymnologicus," citing no less than eight hundred, the laſt one given being a new Sequence, composed in honor of the Virgin in 1855, "Sequentia de Beata Maria Virgine fine Labe Concepta, Virgo Virginum Præclara."

The dispofition of parts in the Mass is as follows, viz.: 1. THE INTROIT, which is the part sung or chanted when the prieſt *enters* within the rails of the altar. 2. THE COLLECT, or PRAYER. 3. READING OF THE EPISTLE, being, in the Mass for the Dead, 1 Cor. xv. 51–57, or Rev. xiv. 13. 4. THE GRADUAL, so called from its having been sung or chanted formerly from the steps (*gradus*) of the altar, closing with the ALLELUIA. 5. THE TRACT, which is omitted when the Alleluia is sung; otherwise it is sung in the interval to prepare for the following. The primary meaning of the word (from *traho*, to protract or draw out) is adapted to suggest either the use here indicated, i. e. to fill up time, or else to express the flow, mournful movement which characterizes the chant. 6. THE SEQUENCE, being, in the Mass for the Dead, the DIES IRÆ. 7. READING OF THE GOSPEL, being, in the Mass for the Dead, John v. 25-29. 8. THE OFFERTORY, which is a short sentence that varies. 9. THE SECRET, a brief prayer recited by the priest in a very low tone of voice. 10. COMMUNION, or the application of the Mass. 11. POST-COMMUNION.

The Sequence, it will be seen, occupies a position exactly midway, being just after the Gradual and Tract, and immediately before the Gospel. The Reading of the Gospel happening to be introduced by the words, "Sequentia Sancti Evangelii secundum ———," (The Continuation of the Holy Gospel according to ———,) some have supposed that the term Sequentia or Sequence was derived from this source. Michael Prætorius was of this opinion. But the moſt approved authorities give the following explanation of its origin.

From an early period, it was the cuſtom of the Latin Church to ſing the Gradual with the Alleluia between the Epiſtle and the Gospel ; the Gradual being completed, the Alleluia followed ; and in order to give to the officiating prieſt or deacon sufficient time to prepare and ascend the ambon or pulpit, the choir repeated and continued the laſt syllable A through a series of notes. This *neuma*, as it was called, or muſical prolongation of a letter, was named SEQUENTIA, because it was sequent to and governed by the melody and rhythm of the Alleluia. At a later period, this paſſage of notes sung without text, conſtituting the original form of the Sequence, came to have words set thereto, thereby preparing the way for other changes ; and forasmuch as the firſt eſſays of this kind were unmetrical in their ſtructure, the term *Prosa* or Prose was applied by way of distinction to this species of compoſition ; of which Notker, surnamed the Stammerer, (Balbulus,) who died in 912, canonized in 1514, is conſidered to have been the originator. Gradually, rhyme, so much and so fondly cultivated in the Middle Ages, found its way into these also ; and from the twelfth century onward, Sequences became proper metrical songs, differing from other hymns only in this, that the ſtrophes, inſtead of four, were made to consist of three or ſix lines, according as they were double or ſingle. To this rule, however, there were some exceptions. The name of Prose, although not ſtrictly proper in its application to metrical compoſitions, continued to be used, nevertheless, as a general title for all Sequences; and so we find the Dies Iræ bearing the appellation in the Mass-books of "Prosa Eccleſiaſtica de Mortuis."

Deſigned in the firſt inſtance, as alleged by Notker, merely to aſſiſt the memory in retaining the longdrawn, caudal melodies of the Alleluia, the deſirableness of having other songs for the Mass than the Gloria in Excelſis, Kyrie, Credo, &c., songs eaſier in ſtructure, which could be joined in, not only by the choir, but also by the congregation,—perhaps, too, the wiſh to introduce greater variety into the service, and bring the ſinging into closer relation with the objects of particular Church feſtivals, which could be done more readily by these Sequences,— caused them to be multiplied greatly.

But the Roman ritual finally limited them to four, viz.: *Victimæ paschali laudis*, S. for Eaſter Sunday;

Veni Sancte Spiritus, S. for Whitsunday and St. Peter's Day; *Lauda Sion Salvatorem*, S. for Solemnity of Corpus Chrifti; and *Dies Iræ*, S. Mass for the Dead and All-Souls' Day; nevertheless, other Mass-books of diocefes and monaftic orders contain more Sequences. The Sequence firft named has a different metre from the other three, being one of those rare cafes in which the characteriftic triplet form of the ftrophe is departed from. The second named, Veni Sancte Spiritus, which Trench speaks of as "the lovelieft, though not the grandeft, of all the hymns in the whole circle of Latin sacred poetry," contains ten ftrophes of three lines each. Its author was Robert the Second, son of Hugh Capet, who ascended the throne of France in the year 997, and died in 1031. Like Henry the Sixth of England, of a meek and gentle dispofition, a lover of peace, he was ill suited to contend with the turbulent and reftless spirits who surrounded him, whose delight was in war. The next Sequence has twelve double ftrophes of fix lines each. It is commonly attributed to the so-called Angelical Doctor, St. Thomas Aquinas. The laft, which is the DIES IRÆ, grand and unapproachable in its excellence, comprises seventeen ftrophes of three lines each, and one of four lines.

ORIGIN OF LATIN RHYME.

WHILE it is true that the Latin hymns written during the firſt centuries of the Chriſtian era are, speaking generally, characterized by the absence of rhyme, and that the prevalence of rhyme belongs peculiarly and almoſt excluſively to the period intervening between the pontificate of Gregory the Great and that of Leo X., it would be a great error to suppose that rhyme was then firſt introduced, or that it was borrowed, as some have surmised, from the Romance or Gothic languages. If we look for its origin, we ſhall find preludings and anticipations of it in every one of the Latin poets, not excepting the oldeſt. Examples of both middle and final rhyme occur in all. In the Introduction to Trench's "Sacred Latin

Poetry," where this whole subject is ably discussed, we have a collation of many of these. Witness the following. An ancient author, quoted by Cicero, (Tusc. l. 1. c. 28,) possibly Ennius, has this —

> Cœlum nitescere, arbores frondescere,
> Vites lætificæ pampinis pubescere,
> Rami baccarum ubertate incurvescere.

Of middle rhyme, we have in Ennius : —

> Non cauponantes bellum, sed belligerantes ;

In Virgil : —

> Limus ut hic durescit, et hæc ut cera liquescit ;

In Ovid : —

> Quem mare carpentem, substrictaque crura gerentem ;

Where also is found this example of leonine pentameter : —

> Quærebant flavos per nemus omne favos.

Of final rhyme, we have, in Virgil : —

> Nec non Tarquinium ejectum Porsenna jubebat
> Accipere, ingentique urbem obsidione premebat ;

Also : —

> Omnis campis diffugit arator,
> Omnis et agricola, et tutâ latet arce viator ;

In Horace: —

> Non satis est pulcra esse poëmata; dulcia sunto,
> Et quocumque volent, animum auditoris agunto;

Also. —

> Multa recedentes adimunt. Ne fortè seniles
> Mandentur juveni partes, pueroque viriles.

Lucan abounds in examples. Even the Latin prosewriters, it would seem, did not disdain now and then to play at rhyme, by putting rhyming words in juxtapofition. Cicero has *florem et colorem*; Pliny, *veram et meram*; Plautus, *melle et felle*; and so others.

Rhyme being thus shown to have been a thing known to the language from the earlieft times, it may be thought surprifing, that what at a later period was so highly prized, and so fondly and so laboriously cultivated, should have been, during so many centuries, to such an extent, neglected; having been apparently fhunned rather than sought for, particularly by those great mafters of poetry who illustrated the Auguftan age. The fact is, that the ancient claffic metres, though found occafionally, as we have seen, toying with rhyme, never seriously affected it; and it was not until the shackles imposed by these had been wholly shaken off, and a simpler and more natural verfification, based upon accent inftead of quantity, had succeeded in eftablifhing its juft claims over the Greek intruder, that the *régime* of rhyme fairly commenced.

Gregorian Chant.

From the "Graduale Romanum."

1. Di - es i - ræ, di - es il - la Sol - vet sæ-clum
2. Quantus tre-mor est fu - tu - rus, Quan-do Ju - dex
7. Quod sum mi - ser tunc dic - tu - rus, Quem pa - tro-num
8. Rex tre - men-dæ ma - jes - ta - tis, Qui sal - van-dos
13. Qui Ma - ri - am ab - sol - vis - ti, Et la - tro-nem
14. Pre-ces me - æ non sunt dig - næ, Sed tu bo - nus

in fa - vil - lâ, Tes - te Da - vid cum Si - byl - la. 3. Tu - ba mi-rum
est ven - tu - rus, Cuncta stric - te dis - cus - su - rus. 4. Mors stu-pe-bit
ro - ga - tu - rus, Cum vix justus sit se - cu - rus? 9. Re - cor - da - re
sal - vas gra - tis, Sal - va me, fons pi - e - ta - tis! 10. Quærens me se-
ex - au - dis - ti, Mi - hi quo-que spem de - dis - ti. 15. In - ter o - ves
fac be - nig - ne, Ne per - en - ni cre - mer ig - ne. 16. Con - fu - ta - tis

spargens so - num Per se - pul-chra re - gi - o - num, Co - get om - nes
et na - tu - ra, Cum re - sur - get cre - a - tu - ra. Ju - di - can - ti
Je - su pi - e, Quod sum cau - sa tu - æ vi - æ, Ne me per - das
dis - ti las - sus, Re - de - mis - ti cru - cem pas - sus: Tan - tus la - bor
lo - cum præ - sta, Et ab hæ - dis me se - questra, Sta - tu - ens in
ma - le - dic - tis, Flammis a - cri - bus ad - dic - tis, Vo - ca me cum

an - te thronum. 5. Li - ber scriptus pro-fe - re - tur, In quo totum
re-spon-su - ra. 6. Ju-dex er - go cum se-de-bit, Quidquid latet
il - lā di - e! 11. Jus-te Ju-dex ul - ti - o - nis, Donum fac re-
not sit cassus! 12. In ge-mis-co tanquam re-us, Cul-pâ ru-bet
par-te dex-trā! 17. O - ro sup-plex et ac-cli - nis, Cor contritum
be - ne - dic-tis!

con - ti - ne-tur, Un-de mundus ju - di - ce-tur.
ap-pa - re - bit, Nil in - ul-tum re-ma - ne-bit.
- mis-si - o-nis An-te di-em ra-ti - o-nis. 18. La-chry-mo-sa
vul-tus me-us: Suppli-can-ti par-ce, De-us!
qua-si ci - nis: Ge-re cu-ram me-i fi - nis!

di - es il - la Qua re - sur-get ex fa - vil - lā, Ju - di - can-dus

ho - mo re - us: Hu - ic er - go par-ce, De - us!

www.ingramcontent.com/pod-product-compliance
Lightning Source LLC
Chambersburg PA
CBHW031408160426
43196CB00007B/939